Unrequited Love

Becca Jane

BookLeaf Publishing

Presentation by *BookLeaf Publishing*

Web: www.bookleafpub.com

E-mail: info@bookleafpub.com

ISBN: 9789357212311

First edition 2023

To the one who listened and taught me how to blend.

ACKNOWLEDGEMENT

Thanks to Hanna and Betty for the unwavering belief.

PREFACE

William Shakespeare's 'Romeo and Juliet' leaves no stone unturned in its description of unrequited love, and it has been a major influence across the course of both my academic and teaching careers.

What can be surmised, albeit simply, from the most influential bard and one of the greatest and darkest love stories of all time is that love returned is nothing short of bliss, love rejected devastating, but love unannounced... well, that brings about a stillness of soul that stagnates and bitterly stops you from living life itself.

Lust

1.
Your eyes have me undone,
The curve of your lip - divine.
The pause as you consider,
The breath we take together.

Lust

2.
Your smile when we meet,
All the words left unsaid.
A promise of tomorrow,
Parting that leaves a depth of sorrow.

Lust

3

3.
Desire runs wild.
I've undressed you a thousand times over.
I'm lost in the thought of you,
A lens of longing is all I see through.

Lust

4.
I push you against a wall,
I trace the path of your neck.
Your breath becomes sharper,
My thoughts of you become darker.

Lust

5

5.
Longing to learn what you desire,
Aching to hear you sigh.
Your lips pressed against mine,
Our bodies entwined.

Lust

6.
You wore blue today,
I remember nothing else.
Undone and rebuilt in a moment,
Rebuilt and yet undone in a moment.

Lust

7.
Conversations that are too brief,
So much left unfinished.
I begin to say that I'm done,
But I see you and become undone.

Love

1.
If I had met you in your summer?
If you had met me in my winter?
Would we be together?
Would it have been forever?

Love

9

2.
We talk about my dreams,
You talk less and less.
Boundaries addressed,
Weeks go by - do I reassess?

Love

3.
Waking dreams of you in my arms. Days filled with your eyes, your smile, your lips, your laugh, your advice, the way you smirk, the way you think, the way you leave your sentences incomplete…

Love

4.
I can't seem to write,
I can't seem to focus…
Why can't you reveal your truth?
What has you so resolute?

Love

12

5.
I go to leave and end this cycle,
You pause, you smile… time idles.
So much is left unsaid,
So much is left unsaid…

Love

6.

Why does love leave you angry?
Why does love leave you lost?
Who takes the first step,
Who is the first to overstep?

Love

7.
The depth of this river is endless,
Our sessions leave me faithless.
You flirt, you beguile, you stay,
I talk, I dream… I'm slain.

Loss

15

1.
The door closes, no one moves,
There is silence and tension.
The pit of emptiness appears,
The road ahead becomes unclear.

Loss

2.
The quiet is disconcerting,
I long to reach out - to connect.
The unenviable task of untangling,
The thought of you still so intermingling.

Loss

3.
I break. I cry, I feel so incomplete.
Why weren't we brave enough to say…
Why weren't we confident enough to stay?
I regret waiting to secure the play.

Loss

4.

Do we share our thoughts?
Do I name you in these lines?
Am I a coward for only contemplating?
Are you weak for all the baiting?

Loss

5.
The seasons change, twist and bend,
My love for you does not end.
The beauty of the sky is reflected in your eyes,
I wish my thoughts of you would lie.

Loss

6.
The beginning of a new chapter,
Time passes and life goes on.
Are we happier apart?
Can we ever be certain of our hearts?

Loss

7.

Lust, love and loss.
Seasons within a year.
No distinct timeline, or end.
Just memories that refuse to blend.

www.ingramcontent.com/pod-product-compliance
Lightning Source LLC
Chambersburg PA
CBHW070733160726
48003CB00006BA/2491